WORLD LEADERS DURING
COVID-19

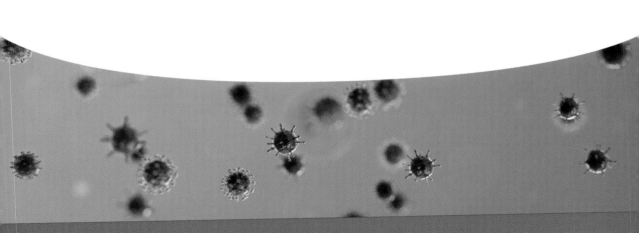

BY DOUGLAS HUSTAD

CONTENT CONSULTANT
Mark N. Lurie, PhD
Associate Professor of Epidemiology, International Health Institute
Brown University School of Public Health

Core Library

An Imprint of Abdo Publishing
abdobooks.com

Cover image: US medical expert Anthony Fauci, *second from left*, gave
regular briefings at the beginning of the COVID-19 pandemic.

abdobooks.com

Published by Abdo Publishing, a division of ABDO, PO Box 398166, Minneapolis, Minnesota 55439. Copyright © 2021 by Abdo Consulting Group, Inc. International copyrights reserved in all countries. No part of this book may be reproduced in any form without written permission from the publisher. Core Library™ is a trademark and logo of Abdo Publishing.

Printed in the United States of America, North Mankato, Minnesota
072020
092020

Cover Photo: Frederic Dides/SIPA/Shutterstock Images
Interior Photos: Shutterstock Images, 4–5; Naohiko Hatta/Kyodo News/AP Images, 9; Taiwan Presidential Office/AP Images, 12–13; Ahn Young-joon/AP Images, 17; Red Line Editorial, 19, 39; Hannah Peters/Getty Images News/Getty Images, 20, 45; Antonio Calanni/AP Images, 22–23, 43; Nicolò Campo/Sipa USA/AP Images, 24; Ugo Amez/Sipa/AP Images, 26; Kay Nietfeld/dpa/AP Images, 28; Patrick Semansky/AP Images, 32–33; Evan Vucci/AP Images, 34

Editor: Marie Pearson
Series Designer: Jake Nordby

Library of Congress Control Number: 2020936515

Publisher's Cataloging-in-Publication Data

Names: Hustad, Douglas, author.
Title: World leaders during COVID-19 / by Douglas Hustad
Description: Minneapolis, Minnesota : Abdo Publishing, 2021 | Series: Core library guide to COVID-19 | Includes online resources and index
Identifiers: ISBN 9781532194085 (lib. bdg.) | ISBN 9781644945056 (pbk.) | ISBN 9781098212995 (ebook)
Subjects: LCSH: Presidents--Juvenile literature. | Center for Disease Control--Juvenile literature. | Governors--Juvenile literature. | Communicable diseases--Prevention--Juvenile literature. | Public health-Juvenile literature. | Epidemics--Juvenile literature. | COVID-19 (Disease)--Juvenile literature.
Classification: DDC 920.00904--dc23

CONTENTS

THE OUTBREAK
IN CHINA

O n February 3, 2020, President Xi Jinping of China addressed some of his country's top leaders. China was going through a crisis. A strange new disease had been spreading since December. Hundreds of people were already dead. Thousands more were infected.

Xi said not to worry. He assured his country's leaders that he was working to contain the problem. The disease did not yet have an official name. It would soon be called COVID-19. Xi said that since January 7, the

Xi Jinping became China's president in 2013.

outbreak had been his top priority. He said he had been giving instructions to local officials on how to handle it. But these instructions had not been given to the public. Xi did not address the public about the virus until January 20. By then, the virus had already spread around the world. The United States had its first reported case the same day.

Just a few days after Xi's speech, Dr. Li Wenliang died of the new virus. Li was one of the first doctors to warn people about COVID-19. He was in Wuhan, China, where the virus was first found. He posted about it on

SARS

The COVID-19 pandemic was not the only major disease to affect China this century. The country had an outbreak of severe acute respiratory syndrome (SARS) in 2002 and 2003. SARS and COVID-19 are very similar. The viruses that cause them both come from a family of viruses called coronaviruses. The SARS outbreak did not infect as many people as COVID-19. The SARS virus infected 8,439 people worldwide. It killed 812.

social media. He wrote his messages on December 30. But the Xi government censored, or blocked, Li's posts. The Chinese government often censors information it does not want discussed publicly. Li's information could have saved lives.

LOCKING DOWN WUHAN

On January 23, the Chinese government issued a strict lockdown for Wuhan. Xi may have limited discussion of the crisis at first. But now his government was acting. Xi called for a national effort to stop the virus. The Chinese government did not want the virus to spread outside Wuhan. It ordered the largest quarantine in human history. The order eventually included 15 cities around Wuhan. That area was home to more than 57 million people.

People were not allowed to travel into or out of the area. Chinese New Year celebrations were canceled. The use of private cars was not allowed. The goal was to keep people away from each other. This would keep

COVID-19 from spreading. The Chinese government tracked people's movements. It required anyone who came from Wuhan to get screened for the virus. The government had always closely monitored its people. Now, that monitoring was even more intense.

THE WORLD WATCHES

The spreading virus got the attention of the World Health Organization (WHO). The WHO is an agency of the United Nations. It advises on public health issues. Its leader was Dr. Tedros Adhanom Ghebreyesus. He was in charge of the WHO's response to COVID-19.

In his native Ethiopia, Tedros had been the minister of health. He had helped the country respond to health issues within its borders. Stopping COVID-19 was an even bigger challenge. Tedros felt it was important to work closely with China. Together, they could help keep the public informed.

Tedros met with Xi on January 28. Tedros was pleased with how China was handling the virus. But he

Tedros, *left*, and Xi shook hands at their January 28 meeting.

knew the virus was spreading outside China. On January 31, Tedros and the WHO declared COVID-19 a global health emergency.

A FRIEND TO CHINA?

On March 11, Tedros and the WHO went further. They declared COVID-19 a pandemic. The disease was spreading quickly around the world. But in China, Xi's government had some success in containing the virus. Tedros praised Xi's efforts.

Tedros felt it was important to keep a good relationship with China. It was where the virus

PERSPECTIVES

ZHAO LIJIAN

Zhao Lijian worked for the Chinese foreign ministry during the COVID-19 pandemic. He suggested COVID-19 did not come from China. Zhao falsely accused the United States of creating the disease. He wrote on Twitter, "It might be US army who brought the epidemic to Wuhan. Be transparent! Make public your data! US owe us an explanation!" Zhao was not alone in spreading conspiracy theories. US senator Tom Cotton suggested the virus could have come from a Chinese lab. Scientists have said that it is very unlikely the virus is human-made.

began spreading. Getting information was vital. But some world leaders criticized Tedros for supporting Xi. They believed China was not telling the truth about the virus. They thought Tedros could have pushed Xi to be more honest.

Xi was not the only world leader challenged by COVID-19. As the disease spread across the globe, government leaders worked to contain the pandemic. Leaders took different approaches. The success of their efforts would be measured by the tragic loss of human lives.

STRAIGHT TO THE
SOURCE

Li Keqiang was the Chinese premier of the state council. He emphasized the importance of working together to stop the virus:

Facing this unexpected disease, the Chinese government has consistently followed a people-centered approach. China puts the life and health of all its people front and center. It has adhered to the principles of shoring up confidence, strengthening unity, following a science-based approach and taking targeted measures, and has all along been open and transparent.

Thanks to the painstaking efforts of the whole country and society, China has achieved major progress in containing the outbreak, and life and work is returning to normal at a faster pace in our country.

Source: "Speech by H. E. Li Keqiang at Special ASEAN Plus Three Summit on COVID-19." *Ministry of Foreign Affairs of the People's Republic of China*, 14 Apr. 2020. fmprc.gov.cn. Accessed 15 June 2020.

WHAT'S THE BIG IDEA?

Take a close look at this statement. What is its main idea? Explain how Li uses evidence to support the main idea.

RESPONSE ACROSS ASIA AND OCEANIA

COVID-19 began spreading outside China in January 2020. The areas closest to China were expected to be most affected at that time. One was Taiwan. This island is southeast of China.

Taiwan had a leader who had handled a pandemic before. Vice President Chen Chien-jen was a disease specialist. He had been Taiwan's head of the Department of Health during the severe acute respiratory syndrome (SARS) outbreak. SARS spread to

In 2016, Tsai Ing-wen, *front*, was elected president of Taiwan. She worked to contain the virus starting in December 2019.

POWER STRUGGLE IN IRAN

In Iran, it was sometimes hard for citizens to tell who was in charge of the COVID-19 response. Iran had a unique government. Supreme Leader Ali Hoseini Khamenei controlled the military. President Hassan Rouhani controlled the government. He led the COVID-19 response. Iran saw its first case in late February. Rouhani said there was no need for lockdowns or quarantines.

In March, Iran was seeing 1,000 new cases per day. Khamenei told the military it could take control of the COVID-19 response if necessary. By March 17, Iran had nearly 1,000 deaths. That was the most deaths in Asia outside China. Later in March, Rouhani ordered a restriction on gatherings.

Taiwan in 2003. Chen had helped contain the SARS virus.

Chen realized that COVID-19 was different from SARS. It spread more easily. He led the effort to make a vaccine and testing kits. He explained to the public the importance of washing hands.

President Tsai Ing-wen also acted quickly. She made a plan even before Taiwan had its first COVID-19 case.

In December, Tsai ordered anyone entering Taiwan from Wuhan be screened for illness.

Taiwan had its first confirmed COVID-19 case on January 21. Tsai called for contact tracing. The government found out where patients had been recently. It located others who may have had contact with a patient. This helped health officials isolate people before they could infect others. Tsai also enforced social distancing, or physical distancing, rules. These rules required people to stay separated from each other.

The government began making masks and other supplies. It needed enough equipment for its people. Tsai called this effort Team Taiwan. Taiwan sent extra supplies to other countries that needed them.

Taiwan kept the spread of COVID-19 within its borders to a minimum. At the end of April, Taiwan had just over 300 active cases. Most of those were people who had traveled from other countries.

By mid-June 2020, Taiwan had fewer than ten active cases. Its total population was 23.6 million.

CASES IN SOUTH KOREA

South Korea was expected to be hit hard by COVID-19. The country is near China. Many people travel between the two countries. People in South Korea remembered the SARS outbreak. Leaders took many of the same early steps as Taiwan.

President Moon Jae-in suggested in February that the virus would quickly disappear. But more and more people got sick. In early March, South Korea had the most COVID-19 cases in the world outside of China. Moon quickly changed his approach. He called for greater testing, isolating sick people, and social distancing.

South Korea had one of the most aggressive testing programs in the world. Tests were widely available to anyone. The government set up drive-through testing centers. People did not even have to leave their cars.

In South Korea, workers sprayed disinfectant in public places as part of the fight against COVID-19.

Testing helped the government understand how many people had the virus. South Korea's case numbers gradually fell.

The government tracked where people with COVID-19 had been through cell phones. Not every country's laws allow them to use this method of contact tracing. But Moon's government was allowed to do so in emergencies. They were able to find people who had been exposed. Those who had been exposed could then quarantine.

These measures helped South Korea respond. As case numbers dropped, the country slowly eased its rules. But cases began to rise again in May. Parts of the country paused reopening.

NEW ZEALAND TAKES NO CHANCES

COVID-19 had spread to nearly every country by the end of February. This included the island nation of New Zealand. Jacinda Ardern led New Zealand's response

WHERE IT BEGAN

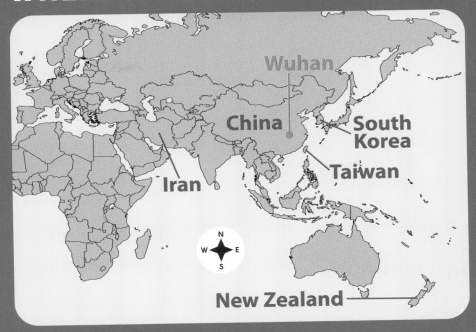

COVID-19 began to spread outward from Wuhan into central China. It eventually spread to larger cities in China and to other parts of the region, such as South Korea and Taiwan. How does this map help you understand the information in this chapter?

to the pandemic. She had been the country's prime minister since 2017.

New Zealand had only a few cases of COVID-19 on March 14. That day Ardern called for strict border control. Anyone entering New Zealand had to be isolated for 14 days. She emphasized social distancing. She ordered more tests.

Ardern regularly appeared on television to give updates. In June she had good news. New Zealand's number of cases had peaked in April. By June 8 it no longer had any active cases. Later some people traveling to New Zealand had the disease. But New Zealand quarantined everyone who came into the country. The chance of it spreading was low.

EXPLORE ONLINE

Chapter Two talks about how Taiwan and South Korea used social distancing policies to keep people from spreading the disease. The website below covers the steps people should take to isolate themselves. Does the article answer any of the questions you had about social distancing?

SOCIAL DISTANCING
abdocorelibrary.com/covid-world-leaders

Jacinda Ardern attends a ceremony after social distancing guidelines were lifted in New Zealand.

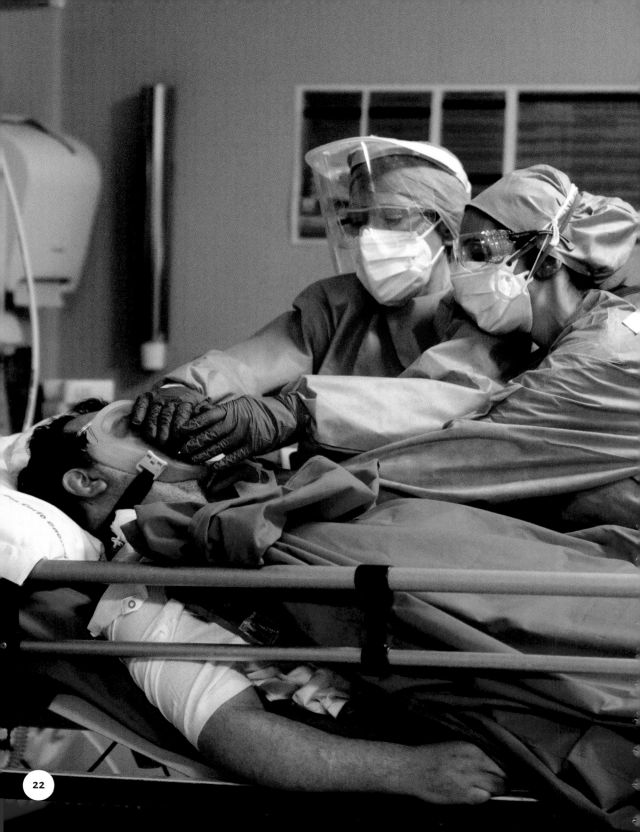

DIFFERENT APPROACHES IN EUROPE

taly was one of the countries hardest hit. It had its first case on January 31. By March 19 it had the most deaths in the world. Some felt this was because Prime Minister Giuseppe Conte was too slow to respond. He stopped all flights to and from China at the end of January. But he did not require lockdowns for everyone right away.

Conte tried to isolate the areas hit hardest. But the virus had already spread. Italy's health

Italian hospitals were quickly filled with COVID-19 patients.

in diretta da **PALAZZO CHIGI**   **Giuseppe Conte**
PRESIDENTE DEL CONSIGLIO

Giuseppe Conte gave televised updates about the lockdowns.

system quickly became overwhelmed. There were too many sick people for all its hospitals to treat.

Conte issued strict measures in early March. People were ordered to stay at home. They needed special permission to travel. Conte urged people to make these sacrifices for the good of the country. These measures were in place for weeks. People faced fines if they broke the rules. Conte told his people to be prepared for the lockdown to last a long time.

Italy's case numbers finally dropped in late April. Some businesses started to open again in May. Italy no longer had the highest number of deaths. But more than 28,000 Italian people had died by May 1. The country had 60 million people.

FIGHTING BACK IN FRANCE

France tracked COVID-19 as it spread in China. But French minister of health Agnès Buzyn said the risk of the virus entering France was low. France had its first confirmed COVID-19 case on January 24. President Emmanuel Macron's government gave basic advice. It said to wash hands and stay away from people. Macron himself did not follow this advice. He visited Italy in February. He shook hands with Conte.

Macron addressed his country on March 12. He admitted France had not been prepared. He told the

Families watched Emmanuel Macron discuss the threat of COVID-19 on March 12.

people that certain businesses would need to close to slow the spread.

France's health-care system was overwhelmed. There were not enough supplies for doctors or beds for patients. Macron increased the country's response in the weeks that followed. He announced a nationwide lockdown on March 16. The number of new cases peaked in early April. They mostly dropped for the rest of the month and into May.

FEWER DEATHS IN GERMANY

Germany had a scientist for its leader during the pandemic. Chancellor Angela Merkel had been a research scientist before becoming a politician. Her background helped her country battle COVID-19.

Germany was one of the hardest-hit nations in Europe. Merkel responded with more testing. She closed public spaces. She explained her decisions to the people. On March 18, she made a televised speech to the nation. Merkel told Germans that COVID-19 was the toughest challenge they had faced since World War II (1939–1945).

Merkel emphasized testing. Germany tested a lot of people. That meant it had a lot of recorded cases. By mid-June, it had a total of 2,245 cases per 1 million people. That was still lower than Italy (3,924) and

Angela Merkel, *left*, and Emmanuel Macron worked together during the COVID-19 pandemic.

France (2,411). At that time, Europe had the highest death rate of any continent. Italy had 568 deaths per 1 million people. France had 451. But Germany was lower at 106. Germany's death rate was among the lowest in the world.

CONFUSION IN THE UNITED KINGDOM

British prime minister Boris Johnson chose a different approach from many other countries at first. He did not use lockdowns. On March 12, he said the country would stop contact tracing. This was against the WHO's advice.

The next day Johnson's chief scientific advisor, Patrick Vallance, spoke on television. He said the country's goal was to develop herd immunity. This concept involves allowing a majority of a population to get an illness. Once people get it, they become immune. They cannot get it again and spread it to more people. If the United Kingdom developed herd immunity, the spread of the virus would

PERSPECTIVES

QUEEN ELIZABETH II

The prime minister is the head of the British government. But the United Kingdom also has a monarch. Historically the king or queen ruled the country. Today monarchs serve ceremonial roles. Queen Elizabeth II is still important to the British people. She played no official role in the COVID-19 response. She did encourage her people, though. She said, "This time we join with all nations across the globe in a common endeavor. Using the great advances of science and our instinctive compassion to heal, we will succeed, and that success will belong to every one of us."

slow down. However, scientists weren't sure if people who had COVID-19 would become immune.

THE SWEDISH APPROACH

Sweden did not issue a lockdown. That was partially the decision of Dr. Anders Tegnell of the Public Health Agency of Sweden. This agency was responsible for Sweden's COVID-19 response. The agency believed keeping society open would lead to herd immunity. For the first few months, Sweden did report fewer deaths than other countries. But by early June, Sweden had more than 4,000 deaths. Neighboring countries Denmark, Norway, and Finland each had fewer than 1,000 deaths. Tegnell admitted in June that the strategy led to too many deaths.

This was never the country's official policy. But Vallance's statement left some citizens confused about what they were supposed to be doing to stay safe. Contact tracing was a way many countries slowed the spread of the virus. Johnson recommended social distancing on March 16. He did not resume contact tracing at that time.

A scientific study in mid-March showed that the death toll in Britain could be worse than previously thought. That prompted Johnson to issue a lockdown order on March 23. This was later than other major European countries. Even after the lockdown, Johnson himself got COVID-19. He had to be hospitalized, but he recovered. In April the United Kingdom announced it would begin contact tracing again.

FURTHER EVIDENCE

Chapter Three discusses herd immunity. Read the article at the website below. Does the information on the website support the information in this chapter? Does it present new information?

HERD IMMUNITY

abdocorelibrary.com/covid-world-leaders

THE WHITE HO

WASHINGTON

MIXED MESSAGES IN THE UNITED STATES

The first case of COVID-19 in the United States was confirmed on January 20. It was in Washington State. The patient had returned from visiting family in Wuhan, China. US president Donald Trump was asked about the threat of the virus days later. He was confident. It was just one person returning from China, he said. The threat to Americans was low.

The Trump administration did take some precautions. On January 31, Trump declared

Donald Trump gave daily briefings on the pandemic during parts of March and April.

Anthony Fauci, *left*, and Deborah Birx, *second from left*, gave Trump advice on how to handle the pandemic.

a public health emergency. He limited entry for people coming in from China. But infected people had already come from other countries.

Trump also made a task force of medical advisers. Among them were Dr. Anthony Fauci and Dr. Deborah Birx. Fauci was the director of the National Institute of Allergy and Infectious Diseases. He had experience with other epidemics, such as HIV/AIDS in the 1980s and

Ebola in 2014. Birx had experience with the US fight against HIV/AIDS.

EARLY STEPS

Fauci and Birx advised Trump. They communicated with the public. Both spoke at press conferences as the virus spread.

The United States had its first COVID-19 death in Washington State on February 29. By mid-March, there were hundreds of new cases per day. Hospitals began reporting a lack of supplies. The United States was not doing as much testing as other countries. That meant it could not know the full scale of cases. Something had to be done to slow the spread of the virus.

Fauci encouraged Trump to promote social distancing. Trump announced those guidelines on March 16. Fauci had pushed for social distancing weeks earlier. He believed it could have saved lives.

By April, evidence showed that wearing masks in public could help slow the spread of the virus.

Fauci then recommended masks. Trump announced this recommendation in a speech. However, Trump also said that he would not wear a mask himself.

CLOSE CALL

The COVID-19 pandemic hit close to home for Canadian prime minister Justin Trudeau. His wife, Sophie, was diagnosed with COVID-19 in March. She had just returned from the United Kingdom. The prime minister isolated himself. He did not get the disease. After his wife recovered, Trudeau kept on working from home as an example of social distancing for the Canadian people.

In May, Trump said that he had been taking the drug hydroxychloroquine. He took it to prevent COVID-19. But there was no evidence it could prevent the disease. The drug had been approved as an emergency treatment in certain cases. But it posed serious risks, including possible heart problems. By June, the drug was no longer approved as a treatment. Medical experts said that people should get medical advice from doctors.

STATES RESPOND

Many US states had trouble getting medical supplies and tests. There was a shortage of tests, masks, and ventilators. In March, hospitals in New York were filling up. Medical workers didn't have enough personal protective gear, such as masks. Hospitals ran out of room to hold the bodies of those who had passed. They used refrigerated trucks to hold more until funeral homes could take them. Governors asked the federal government to help provide emergency equipment for their states. Soon the federal stockpile of supplies was nearly drained. Trump said states should then buy supplies themselves. But that set up competition among states. They tried to outbid each other in order to buy supplies from companies.

It took time for states to get what they needed. States had to start making their own plans in March. There was no official federal plan. Trump gave some guidance in April. But it was up to each state to make its own decisions and guidelines for its residents.

THE CONTINUING THREAT

Trump stayed confident about his country's COVID-19 response into May. He started planning for the days when life could gradually return to normal. Trump held a rally for his reelection in Tulsa, Oklahoma, in June. The US Centers for Disease Control and Prevention still recommended social distancing. But rally attendees were not asked to do so.

By July, the United States had surpassed 131,000 deaths. It had 40.19 deaths per 100,000 people.

PERSPECTIVES

JAIR BOLSONARO

Jair Bolsonaro was president of Brazil during the pandemic. State governors began closing businesses for a lockdown in March. Bolsonaro felt that went too far. He didn't think slowing the spread of the virus was worth hurting Brazil's economy. He said, "We should take steps, the virus could turn into a fairly serious issue. But the economy has to function because we can't have a wave of unemployment." By mid-June, Brazil had more deaths than any other country besides the United States. Bolsonaro tested positive for COVID-19 in July.

COVID-19 DEATHS
BY COUNTRY

This graph shows the total deaths per 100,000 people by July 8, 2020, for several countries discussed in this book. Why do you think some countries had a higher death rate than others?

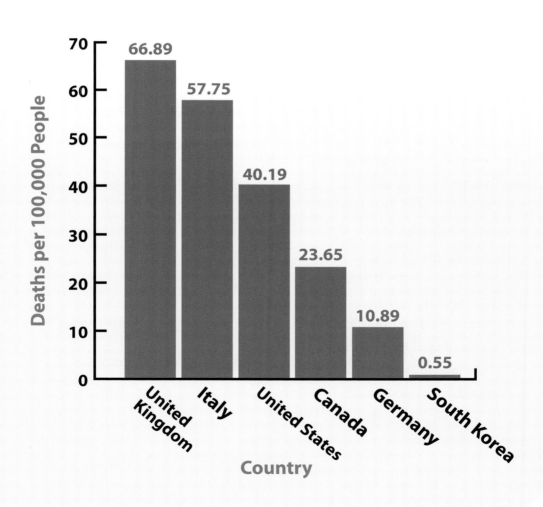

Deaths per 100,000 People

- United Kingdom: 66.89
- Italy: 57.75
- United States: 40.19
- Canada: 23.65
- Germany: 10.89
- South Korea: 0.55

Country

That was higher than neighboring countries Canada and Mexico. But it was lower than the United Kingdom, Spain, Italy, and France. Fauci and other experts believed if the United States had taken precautions earlier, it could have had fewer deaths. Experts also believed that a clear, consistent message at the federal level would have led to fewer cases. Trump had encouraged reopening in May. Many states began reopening in May and June. COVID-19 cases then started rising. States had to pause their reopening plans. At the same time, new cases in Europe had dropped significantly.

The COVID-19 pandemic caught many world leaders off guard. Those who acted early were more likely to keep their case numbers low. But many discovered their countries were unprepared for a pandemic. The lessons they learned from COVID-19 would help prepare other world leaders in the future.

STRAIGHT TO THE
SOURCE

One of the decisions many world leaders struggled with was whether or not to issue a lockdown. People had to be kept safe from the virus. But lockdowns also caused many people to lose their jobs. Trump was one leader who worried that the lockdown would cause more harm than good:

> So let me be extremely clear about one point: We will move heaven and earth to safeguard our great American citizens. We will continue to use every power, every authority, every single resource we've got to keep our people healthy, safe, secure, and to get this thing over with. We want to finish this war. We have to get back to work. . . . We have to open our country again. We don't want to be doing this for months and months and months. We're going to open our country again. This country wasn't meant for this. Few were.

> Source: "Remarks by President Trump, Vice President Pence, and Members of the Coronavirus Task Force." *White House*, 5 Apr. 2020. whitehouse.gov. Accessed 1 May 2020.

CHANGING MINDS

Imagine you are a world leader like Trump. How would you argue for or against ending lockdowns sooner? Make sure you explain your opinion. Include facts and details to support your reasons.

FAST FACTS

- The virus that causes the disease COVID-19 began spreading in China in December 2019. President Xi Jinping of China at first tried to control the spread of information about the virus, only later reporting it publicly.

- World Health Organization leader Dr. Tedros Adhanom Ghebreyesus traveled to China early to monitor the situation. He praised Xi's efforts to contain the virus through a lockdown.

- Taiwan saw cases early on in the pandemic. President Tsai Ing-wen took steps to limit travel from China before Taiwan had its first confirmed case. Vice president Chen Chien-jen provided expertise from his previous management of the SARS epidemic.

- South Korean president Moon Jae-in's expanded testing policies helped his country shrink its case numbers, which were once the second-most in the world.

- Italy was one of the hardest-hit countries in Europe. Prime Minister Giuseppe Conte was forced to take aggressive actions after his country experienced a large spike in cases and deaths.

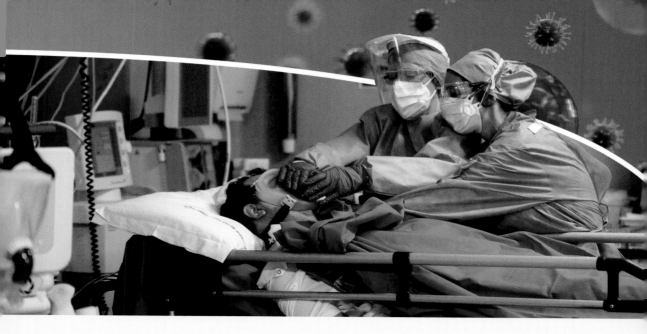

- German chancellor Angela Merkel used her science background to evaluate the best course of action for her country, helping it have one of the lowest death rates in Europe.

- United Kingdom prime minister Boris Johnson hoped to minimize lockdowns and slow the spread of the virus, but he was forced to quickly tighten the country's restrictions. Johnson himself contracted COVID-19 but recovered.

- US president Donald Trump limited travel from China at the end of January. The federal government did not have enough medical supplies or tests early on in the pandemic, leaving states to make their own plans.

- Doctors Anthony Fauci and Deborah Birx served on a task force to advise the president. They encouraged Trump to promote social distancing to help slow the spread of the virus.

STOP AND
THINK

Tell the Tale

World leaders took a variety of approaches in responding to the COVID-19 pandemic. Imagine you are a health expert asked to give some advice to the people of your country. What basic facts would you want them to know? Write a short speech of 200 words.

Surprise Me

This book discusses some of the different strategies world leaders took in responding to COVID-19. After reading this book, what two or three facts did you find the most surprising? Write a few sentences about each one. Why did you find these facts surprising?

Dig Deeper

After reading this book, what questions do you still have about world leaders during the COVID-19 pandemic? With an adult's help, find a few reliable sources that can help you answer your questions. Write a paragraph about what you learned.

Say What?

Studying a pandemic can mean learning a lot of new vocabulary. Find five words in this book you've never heard before. Use a dictionary to find out what they mean. Then write the meanings in your own words and use each word in a sentence.

GLOSSARY

administration
a group of people in charge
of something

ceremonial
reserved for purposes that
do not have real power
or influence

conspiracy theory
an idea that the truth about
something is different than
the official explanation

economy
a system of making and
selling products and
providing services

epidemic
a disease that has spread to
many people in a large area

immunity
being protected from getting
a certain disease

minister
a title for a government
official in some countries

pandemic
a disease that spreads across
the world

quarantine
a separated space from
others to avoid spreading
a disease

ventilator
a medical device that helps
people breathe

ONLINE
RESOURCES

To learn more about world leaders during COVID-19, visit our free resource websites below.

Visit **abdocorelibrary.com** or scan this QR code for free Common Core resources for teachers and students, including vetted activities, multimedia, and booklinks, for deeper subject comprehension.

Visit **abdobooklinks.com** or scan this QR code for free additional online weblinks for further learning. These links are routinely monitored and updated to provide the most current information available.

LEARN
MORE

Hinman, Bonnie. *Donald Trump: 45th President of the United States*. Abdo Publishing, 2018.

London, Martha. *The Spread of COVID-19*. Abdo Publishing, 2021.

INDEX

About the Author

Douglas Hustad is a freelance writer and author of dozens of science and history books for young people. He and his family live in northern San Diego County.